100 BLACKBOARD GAMES REVISED

by Les Landin

Fearon Teacher Aids
A Divison of Frank Schaffer Publications, Inc.

Editorial Director: Virginia L. Murphy
Editor: Kristin Eclov
Illustration: Teena Remer
Cover and Inside Design: Rose Sheifer

This Fearon Teacher Aids product was formerly manufactured and distributed
by American Teaching Aids, Inc., a subsidiary of Silver Burdett Ginn, and is
now manufactured and distributed by Frank Schaffer Publications, Inc.
FEARON, FEARON TEACHER AIDS and the FEARON balloon logo are
marks used under license from Simon & Schuster, Inc.

ISBN: 0-86653-919-0

Printed in the United States of America
1. 15 14

Introduction

This book contains a collection of blackboard games contributed by teachers who have attended my blackboard-techniques classes at San Jose State College. The teachers picked their favorite games that were used regularly in their classrooms. Some of the games were created by elementary school children. They have all been tried in primary- or intermediate-grade classrooms and have proven to be both entertaining and educational. The book contains both competitive and noncompetitive games thereby allowing the teacher to choose activities that suit his or her class. Teachers will find that a number of the primary-grade games can be used at the intermediate-grade level if modified to meet the needs of the older children. In the same sense, a number of the intermediate-grade games can also be adapted for the primary-grade level.

Contents

<u>TOOTHY</u>

A Primary Game for Health, Reading, Social Studies, Math, Spelling, and Language

1. HEALTH TOOTHY: Draw a face with five large teeth showing. Toothy always forgets to brush her teeth. The class is going to show Toothy how to clean them.

2. The teacher asks a child a question about health.

3. If the child answers the question correctly he or she can come up and color one of Toothy's teeth with white chalk. (White teeth represent well-brushed teeth.)

4. Children are given turns answering questions until all of Toothy's teeth are white.

5. READING TOOTHY: Played the same, except that children are given questions to answer from their reading skills instruction.

6. SOCIAL STUDIES TOOTHY: Children are given social studies questions to answer.

7. MATH TOOTHY: Children are given math problems to solve.

8. SPELLING TOOTHY: Children are given spelling words to spell.

9. LANGUAGE TOOTHY: Children are given vocabulary words to pronounce.

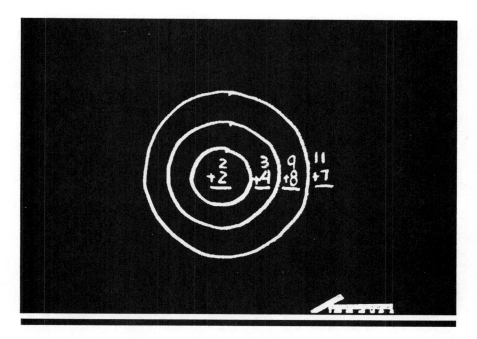

HIT THE TARGET

A Primary Game for Spelling, Language, Math,
and Social Studies

1. MATH HIT THE TARGET: Draw three circles, one inside the other on the blackboard.

2. A child is chosen to stand ten to twenty feet (3.1 m to 6.1 m) from the target. The distance is based on the age and skill of the child.

3. The child is given an eraser or bean bag to throw at the target.

4. The child must solve the problem within the circle he or she hits.

5. One point is given for each correct answer.

6. The inner circle contains the easiest math problem. The problems become more difficult with each larger circle. If a child completely misses the target, he or she should solve the problem outside the largest circle.

7. The children often aim for the center of the target because the problems are easier and they can earn more points. The teacher should change the problems fairly often in order to challenge the children.

8. LANGUAGE HIT THE TARGET: Played the same, except that words are placed on the target instead of math problems. Children must pronounce the word inside the circle they hit. The easier words should be placed towards the center of the target.

9. SPELLING HIT THE TARGET: Played the same, except that letters are placed on the target. Children must spell words from their spelling lists that begin with the letter they hit. Letters of easier words should be placed towards the target's center.

10. SOCIAL STUDIES HIT THE TARGET: Place numbers on the target that correspond to dates or questions in the social studies book. Easier questions should be placed towards the center of the target.

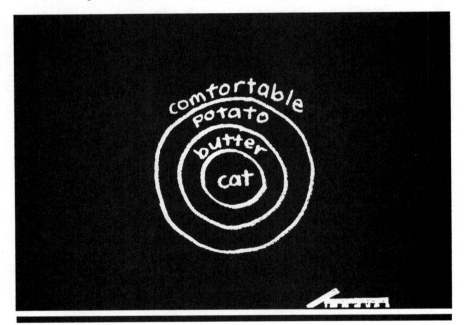

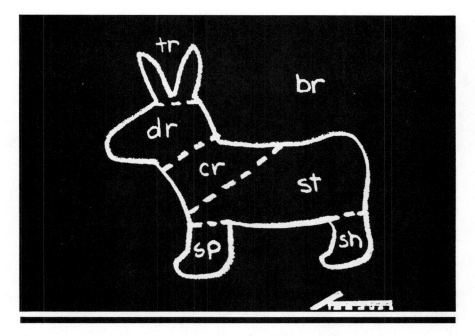

DRAW THE TAIL ON THE DONKEY

A Primary Game for Reading, Math, and Language

1. LANGUAGE DRAW THE TAIL: Draw a large donkey on the blackboard.
2. Write starting sounds on various sections of the donkey as shown in the illustration.
3. Choose a child and bring him or her to a spot a few feet (m) from the donkey.
4. Blindfold the child and give him or her a piece of chalk.
5. Lead the child to the donkey. Encourage the child to draw a tail on the picture.
6. Remove the blindfold. The child must say a word beginning with the starting sound in the section he or she has marked. If the child completely misses the donkey, he or she should use the starting sound on the outside of the picture.
7. If the child correctly uses the starting sound, he or she can call another child to come up to the blackboard.

8. MATH DRAW THE TAIL: Played the same, except that numbers are written inside the donkey. Children must read the numbers. Children can give the numbers before and after the number written inside the donkey. Math problems can also be written in the sections.

9. READING DRAW THE TAIL: Write words from the vocabulary list on the donkey. The children will read the word from the section of the donkey they hit. Encourage children to define the vocabulary words, too.

PEEK-A-BOO

A Primary Game for Reading, Language, and Math

1. LANGUAGE PEEK-A-BOO: Cut a clown's head out of cardboard. This is Peek-A-Boo.

2. The clown face can be used to cover short sentences written on the blackboard. The sentences can be written in the form of simple commands.

3. The teacher says, "Peek-A-Boo says . . ." and he or she quickly uncovers the short sentence on the board. Cover the sentence again after two to four seconds (the time will vary with the age of the children).

4. The teacher calls on one child to follow the command.

5. MATH PEEK-A-BOO: Played the same, except that children must read the numbers or solve short math problems hidden behind Peek-A-Boo's face.

6. READING PEEK-A-BOO: Starting sounds or vocabulary words are hidden behind Peek-A-Boo. Have the children practice pronouncing the vocabulary words or write new words using the starting sounds.

7. These games can also be played with two teams. Children can write words on index cards and use Peek-A-Boo as cover when giving words to each other.

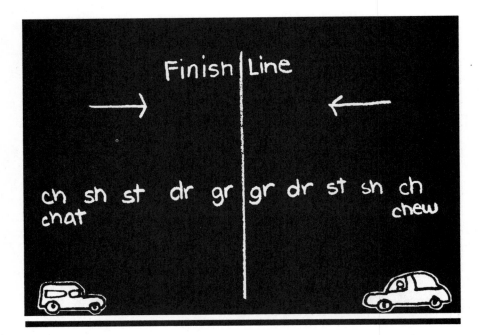

BLACKBOARD AUTO RACES

A Primary Game for Math, Spelling, and Reading

1. READING AUTO RACES: Children draw and cut out their own cardboard cars (or horses, turtles, or ships) before the game. Remind children to draw on both sides of the cars.

2. Two children are chosen to bring their cars up to the blackboard.

3. The two cars are placed at opposite ends of the chalk tray.

4. Write five starting sounds on both sides of the blackboard finish line as shown above.

5. Have each child stand in front of his or her first starting sound. The car should be located on the chalk tray directly below the starting sound.

6. The teacher gives the starting signal and the children race to the center finish line. Each child must make a word out of the starting sound before moving his or her car to the next sound.

7. The first car to reach the finish line is the winner.

8. SPELLING AUTO RACES: Write five incorrectly spelled words on each side of the finish line. Children race to the finish line after correctly spelling each word.

9. MATH AUTO RACES: Write five math problems on each side of the finish line. Children race to the finish line as they correctly solve each math problem.

Finish | Line

$\rightarrow$ $\leftarrow$

$\begin{array}{r}2\\+2\\\hline 4\end{array}$ $\begin{array}{r}3\\+3\\\hline\end{array}$ $\begin{array}{r}5\\+4\\\hline\end{array}$ $\begin{array}{r}3\\+4\\\hline\end{array}$ $\begin{array}{r}3\\+5\\\hline\end{array}$ $\begin{array}{r}3\\+5\\\hline\end{array}$ $\begin{array}{r}3\\+4\\\hline\end{array}$ $\begin{array}{r}5\\+4\\\hline\end{array}$ $\begin{array}{r}3\\+3\\\hline\end{array}$ $\begin{array}{r}2\\+2\\\hline 4\end{array}$

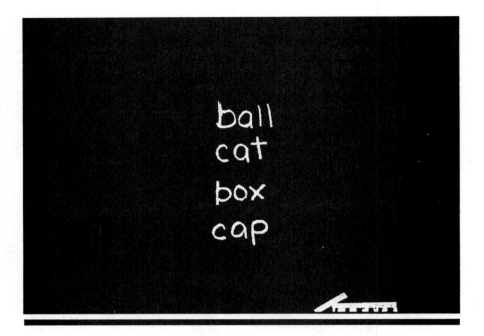

BEHIND YOUR BACK

A Primary Game for Reading, Spelling, Social Studies, Language, and Math

1. READING BEHIND YOUR BACK: The teacher writes four vocabulary words on the blackboard.

2. A child is chosen to stand with his or her back to the board in front of the class.

3. Another child is chosen to come up and point to one of the words for the class to see.

4. The class pronounces the word silently for the child with his or her back to the board. He or she must guess the word the children are pronouncing.

5. If the child guesses the correct word, he or she can be the one to point out the next word.

6. ARITHMETIC BEHIND YOUR BACK: Played the same, except that numbers are written on the board.

7. SPELLING BEHIND YOUR BACK: Spelling words are listed on the board. The child must spell the word the class is pronouncing.

8. SOCIAL STUDIES BEHIND YOUR BACK: Names of famous people or places are written on the board. The child must figure out the name the class is pronouncing.

9. LANGUAGE BEHIND YOUR BACK: Vocabulary words are written on the board. The child must divide the word into syllables and then correctly pronounce it.

STOP THE PIRATES

A Primary Game for Spelling, Reading, Math, and Social Studies

1. SPELLING STOP THE PIRATES: The teacher draws five treasure chests on an island. Between the island and a pirate ship the teacher draws five waves. The water is keeping the pirates from reaching the island and the treasure.

2. Divide the class into two teams—Pirates and Guards. The Pirates want to take the treasure and the Guards want to hide it.

3. The teacher gives a spelling word to the first Pirate. If the Pirate spells the word correctly, he or she can erase one wave. If the word is misspelled, no waves can be erased.

4. Next, the teacher gives a word to the first Guard. If the Guard spells the word correctly, one treasure chest can be buried.

5. The object of the game is for the Pirates to remove the five waves of water before the Guards can bury the five treasure chests.

6. SOCIAL STUDIES STOP THE PIRATES: The treasure and pirates can be replaced with characters in history. For example, Davy Crockett can be trying to cross five stepping stones in a creek to reach five raccoons who are trying to hide in a tree. The teacher asks history questions instead of spelling words.

7. MATH STOP THE PIRATES: Played the same, except the teacher asks the players to solve math problems at the blackboard.

8. READING STOP THE PIRATES: The Guards and Pirates can be replaced with characters from a book the class is reading. The children are given vocabulary words to define.

OBSTACLE COURSE

A Primary Game for Spelling, Social Studies,
Reading, Science, Language, and Math

1. SPELLING OBSTACLE COURSE: The class is divided into two lines.

2. Each line stands 15 to 20 feet (4.6 m to 6.1 m) from the blackboard.

3. The children are told to hop, skip, walk backwards or blindfolded to the blackboard when given the starting signal.

4. The teacher gives a spelling word to be written on the blackboard. This is the starting signal.

5. The first two children hop to the blackboard, write the word and hop back to the end of their lines.

6. The next two children are given words.

7. The line with the most correctly spelled words on the blackboard is the winner.

8. SOCIAL STUDIES OBSTACLE COURSE: Played the same, except the children answer social studies questions on the board.

9. READING OBSTACLE COURSE: Children are given questions from their reading skills instruction.

10. SCIENCE OBSTACLE COURSE: Children are given science questions.

11. LANGUAGE OBSTACLE COURSE: Children are given definitions for vocabulary words. The children must write the words next to the definitions on the blackboard.

12. MATH OBSTACLE COURSE: Children are given tables or math problems to answer on the board.

13. STOP-GO OBSTACLE COURSE: This game can be played the same as language or math. As children start racing to the board, the teacher calls out, "Stop!" The children must stop where they are even if they have started writing or working the problem on the board. The teacher then says, "Go!" and the racers proceed. The race continues as the teacher gives the surprise commands of "Stop" and "Go."

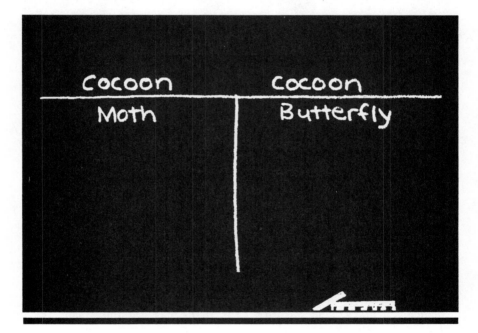

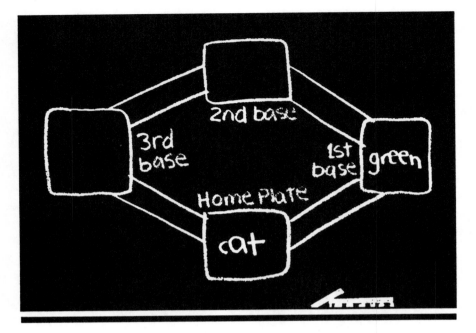

BLACKBOARD BASEBALL

A Primary- and Intermediate-Grade Game for Math, Language, Science, Social Studies, Spelling, and Reading

1. SPELLING BASEBALL: Draw home plate and three bases on the blackboard as shown in the illustration.

2. Divide the room into two sides and let the children choose names for their teams. For example, the Yankees and the Dodgers.

3. The Yankees can be "up" first. The first child on the Yankee team walks up to the chalkboard.

4. The teacher or a student says, "Here's the windup, the pitch, and the ball is . . ." and a spelling word is given to the player at home plate.

5. The player writes the word on home plate. If the word is spelled correctly, he or she can go to first base.

6. The next Yankee player comes up to the plate and waits for the next "pitch."

7. The teacher gives another spelling word. Both children write the words on their bases.

8. If both children spell their words correctly, they move on to the next bases just as in regular baseball.

9. If a child misses a word he or she must sit down. This is an "out." The other players continue around the bases.

10. After the Yankees have made three outs, the Dodgers are up to bat.

11. Each time a child is able to move through the four squares, his or her team is given one run. Keep track of the runs and the outs.

12. MATH BASEBALL: Played the same, except the children are given math problems to solve at each base.

13. LANGUAGE BASEBALL: Children are given definitions for vocabulary words. The children should write the word that fits the definition on the base.

14. SCIENCE BASEBALL: Children are given categories, such as insects, minerals, plants, and so on. On each base, have children write an item that fits the category.

15. SOCIAL STUDIES BASEBALL: Children are given categories, such as countries, wars, inventors, and so on. To move to the next base, have the children write an item from that category on their base.

16. READING BASEBALL: Children are given descriptions of characters taken from books they read in class. Children should write the names of characters on the bases.

CONSTRUCTION CREWS

A Primary- and Intermediate-Grade Game for Sentence Construction, Punctuation, and Word Review

1. DRAWING CONSTRUCTION CREW: Divide the class into two teams, for example, the Carpenters and the Architects.

2. The two teams form two lines in front of the blackboard.

3. The first players in each line go to the blackboard. Each child draws a line and goes back to the end of his or her line.

4. The next two players each add one line, then the third set of players each add their own lines.

5. The object is to see which team can draw the best picture. The class can vote on the winner.

6. WORD CONSTRUCTION CREW: Played the same, except the children must build a complete word. The first child in each line writes any letter he or she chooses on the board. Each child can add only one letter to make the word. The winning word must have the same number of letters as children in line. Letters can be added to the beginning or ending of the word.

7. SENTENCE CONSTRUCTION CREW: Played the same, except that the children must build a sentence with the correct punctuation. The first child in each line can write any word he or she wishes on the blackboard. Each child can add only one word to the sentence. The last child in line is responsible for punctuation. The winning sentence must have the same number of words as children in line. Words can be added to the beginning or ending of the sentence.

CATS AND DOGS

A Primary- and Intermediate-Grade Game for Social Studies, Reading, Language, Spelling, Math, and Science

1. SPELLING CATS AND DOGS: The teacher draws a tic-tac-toe game on the blackboard as shown in the illustration.

2. Divide the class into two teams.

3. Children can choose their own symbols for the game. For example, dogs and cats.

4. The teacher gives the first child on the cat's team a spelling word.

5. If the child spells the word correctly, he or she can draw a cat in a square. If the word is spelled incorrectly, no mark can be made.

6. The dog team takes a turn.

7. The game continues until one side or the other has a straight row of dogs or cats in a horizontal, vertical, or diagonal line.

8. MATH CATS AND DOGS: Children are given math problems to work instead of spelling words.

9. READING CATS AND DOGS: Children are given vocabulary words to define.

10. SOCIAL STUDIES CATS AND DOGS: Children are given social studies questions to answer.

11. SCIENCE CATS AND DOGS: Children are given science questions to answer.

12. LANGUAGE CATS AND DOGS: Children are shown words that they must pronounce correctly. The words can be taken out of reading or social studies materials.

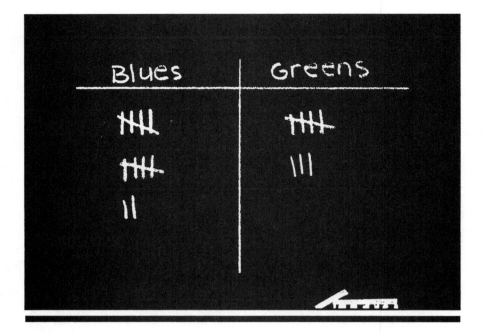

HOLE IN ONE

A Primary- and Intermediate-Grade Game for Social Studies, Science, Language, Math, and Spelling

1. SOCIAL STUDIES HOLE IN ONE: The class is divided into two teams, for example, Blues and Greens.

2. The first child on the Blues team stands ten to twenty feet (3.1 m to 6.1 m) from the trash can. The distance may vary based on the age and skill level of the children. The child from the Blue team tries to throw an eraser into the trash can.

3. If the eraser goes into the can, the Blue team can ask him or her a question about social studies.

4. If the eraser misses the trash can, the Green team can ask a social studies question.

5. It is important for the player to hit the can because his or her own team will ask easier questions. Any child who asks a question, however, must know the answer.

6. The game continues as the first Green player has his or her turn at making a basket. One point is scored for each correct answer.

7. SCIENCE HOLE IN ONE: Played the same, except the questions are taken from the science text.

8. MATH HOLE IN ONE: Children are given math problems to solve.

9. LANGUAGE HOLE IN ONE: Children are given vocabulary words to define.

10. SPELLING HOLE IN ONE: Children are given spelling words to spell.

sh ch dr tr br st

SHUFFLE BLACKBOARD

**A Primary- and Intermediate-Grade Game for Reading,
Math, Language, and Spelling**

1. LANGUAGE SHUFFLE BLACKBOARD: Write six or more starting sounds across the blackboard.

2. A child is chosen to stand at one end of the chalk tray.

3. At a given signal, he or she slides the eraser along the tray.

4. The child must pronounce a word beginning with each starting sound above the eraser.

5. MATH SHUFFLE BLACKBOARD: Played the same, except the child must solve each math problem written on the blackboard.

6. READING SHUFFLE BLACKBOARD: Played the same, except the child must define each vocabulary word taken from the reading skills instruction.

7. SPELLING SHUFFLE BLACKBOARD: Letters are written along the blackboard. The child must spell a word from the spelling list that begins with each letter on the board.

SECRET CODE

An Intermediate-Grade Game for Language, Reading, Math, and Social Studies

1. LANGUAGE SECRET CODE: Divide the class into two teams, the Secret Agents and the Spies.

2. The first Spy walks to the board and writes a "secret code" command to his or her team. The Spies must guess the meaning of the command before the Secret Agents.

3. The team that acts out the command first wins the round. Now it's the Secret Agents' turn to write a "secret code" command on the board.

4. The message must be no longer than six words and must involve a command that the team can carry out in the room.

5. READING SECRET CODE: Played the same, except that players write scrambled words taken from the reading skills instruction. Players must unscramble each word. For example, egarl (answer: large).

6. MATH SECRET CODE: Players write scrambled math problems with correct answers on the blackboard. Example: 2 + 2 - 4 = 4 (answer: 4 + 2 - 2 = 4).

7. SOCIAL STUDIES SECRET CODE: Players write scrambled sentences stating history facts or sayings. For example, fight only I have begun to (answer: "I have only begun to fight.").

BLACKBOARD SPIN THE BOTTLE

An Intermediate-Grade Game for Language, Social Studies, Science, and Math

1. MATH SPIN THE BOTTLE: Five children are chosen to stand underneath the five numbers written on the blackboard. The children are referred to as "bottles."

2. Children spin the "bottles" by calling out multiples of the numbers on the blackboard.

3. When a child hears a multiple of his or her number, the child quickly spins around once. For example, if the number 25 is called the child under the number 5 spins around once.

4. If a child fails to spin when a multiple of his or her number is called, that child must exchange places with another child in the class.

5. LANGUAGE SPIN THE BOTTLE: Played the same, except that children or "bottles" stand under various starting sounds, such as ch, st, dr, and so on. When the class calls out a word with a child's starting sound he or she must spin around once.

6. HISTORY SPIN THE BOTTLE: Played the same, except that children stand under various categories of history, such as presidents, wars,

inventors, and so on. When the class calls out an item from a child's category he or she must spin.

7. GEOGRAPHY SPIN THE BOTTLE: Played the same, except children stand under various categories of geography, such as rivers, cities, countries, and so on.

8. SCIENCE SPIN THE BOTTLE: Played the same, except children stand under various categories of science, such as minerals, planets, insects, and so on.

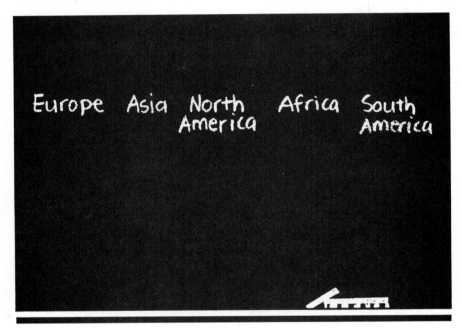

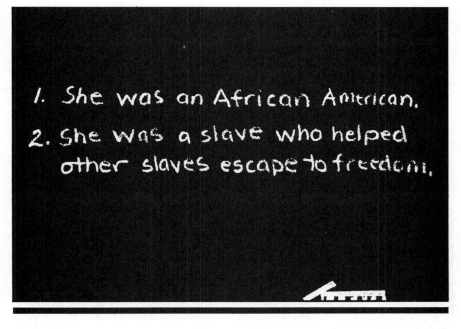

1. She was an African American.
2. She was a slave who helped other slaves escape to freedom.

MS. "E"

An Intermediate-Grade Game for Social Studies, Reading, and Language

1. MS. E'S HISTORY GAME: A child is chosen to go to the blackboard with his or her social studies book.

2. The child thinks of a famous person in history. He or she says, "Ms. E helped establish the Underground Railroad. Who was she?" (answer: Harriet Tubman).

3. The class tries to guess the identity of Ms. E by asking questions, such as "What was she known for?," What did she look like?," and so on.

4. The child at the board must answer his or her classmates' questions by writing complete sentences on the board as shown above. The child cannot answer any question orally.

5. This game can also be played with two teams. Each team can choose a character from history for the other team to guess.

6. MS. E'S GEOGRAPHY GAME: The child at the board thinks of a mystery mountain, city, river, or country that Ms. E is visiting. The game continues in the same way as described above.

7. MS. E'S READING GAME: The child at the board thinks of a mystery story or book that Ms. E. is reading. The story should be from a book the class is reading together.

8. MS. E'S SPELLING GAME. The child at the board thinks of a mystery word from the spelling list. The child at the board should only give the first letter of the mystery word.

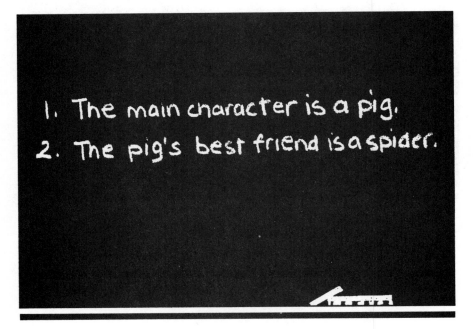

1. The main character is a pig.
2. The pig's best friend is a spider.

BLACKBOARD FOOTBALL

An Intermediate-Grade Game for Science, Reading, Social Studies, Spelling, Math, and Language

1. SPELLING FOOTBALL: Divide the class into two teams, for example, the Bears and the Giants.

2. A player from the Giants is given a word to spell. If he or she spells it correctly, the football is moved over the Bear's 40-yard line. Each time the ball is moved it is redrawn along the football field.

3. A Bears' player is given a word. If he or she spells it correctly, the ball is moved back ten yards to the 50-yard line. Now it is the Giants' turn.

4. If a player on either team spells a word incorrectly, the ball does not move.

5. The first team that reaches the opponent's goal line has made a touchdown and receives six points.

6. Keep track of the score as shown in the illustration.

7. MATH FOOTBALL: Played the same, except the teacher gives the team members math problems to solve on the board.

8. SOCIAL STUDIES FOOTBALL: Played the same, except the teams answer social studies questions.

9. SCIENCE FOOTBALL: The teacher gives the students science questions to answer.

10. READING FOOTBALL: The teacher gives vocabulary words to define or reading questions to answer from the daily reading work.

11. LANGUAGE FOOTBALL: Played the same, except the teacher gives the players words to pronounce correctly.

Winner

ch	sh	dr	tr
chow	shot	drive	train
chat	sheet	drag	trap
chew		drop	tramp
chip		drill	tree
		drip	

BLACKBOARD RELAYS

**An Intermediate-Grade Game for Reading, Math,
Language, Science, and Social Studies**

1. READING RELAYS: Divide the class into four relay lines of five children each. The size can vary depending on the number of children playing.

2. Write four starting sounds on the blackboard.

3. The four relay lines should stand in front of the four starting sounds.

4. At a given signal, the first child in each line runs up to the board and writes one word using the starting sound. He or she then hands the chalk to the next child and sits at the end of the line.

5. The next child writes a word in the same manner and the race continues until one line is completely seated. If all the children in that line have used the starting sound correctly, they are the winners of the race.

6. GEOGRAPHY RELAYS: Children race to list the items in categories, such as famous places, rivers, mountains, cities, and so on.

7. HISTORY RELAYS: Children race to list items in categories, such as famous inventors, authors, presidents, and so on.

8. SCIENCE RELAYS: Children race to list items in categories, such as plants, endangered species, insects, and so on.

9. LANGUAGE RELAYS: Children race to list items in categories, such as parts of speech, 1st, 2nd, and 3rd person, plural and singular classifications, and so on.

10. MATH RELAYS: Children race to list multiples of numbers.

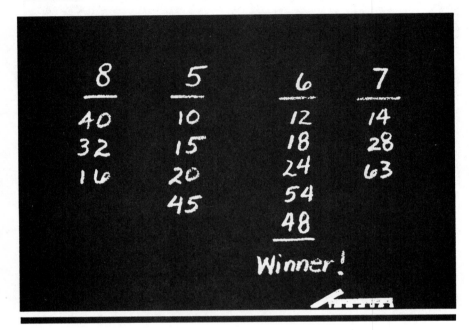

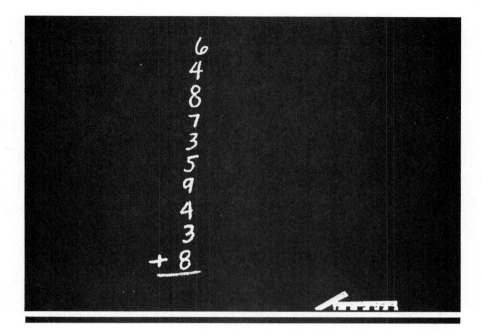

BEAT YOURSELF

An Intermediate-Grade Game for Math, Social Studies, and Keeping Desks Clean

1. MATH BEAT YOURSELF: The teacher writes a column of numbers on the blackboard.

2. At the exact moment when the second hand on the classroom's clock is up, the children start adding the column of numbers mentally. As soon as they have the answer, have the children look at the clock and write down their own individual times. Remind the children to not share their times with anyone.

3. The teacher waits until all of the children have finished adding and then announces the correct answer. Children that have the wrong answer should erase their marked time. Children that have the correct answer should record their time to see if they can do better the next day.

4. If the room does not have a clock, the teacher may want to bring in a cooking timer for the children to use.

5. Children should keep records of their times and dates so they can see their own improvement during the year.

6. This game can also be played with subtraction, multiplication, division, and fraction problems. The number of problems should stay the same but the level of difficulty can change slightly.

7. In presenting a subtraction column, the teacher should start with a large number and subtract from it. Example: 92 - 8 - 4 - 9 = ?

8. In presenting math problems, a certain number of multiplication and division problems should be written on the blackboard. Example: 4 X 5 = ?, 7 X 8 = ? Have the children mark their times when they have completed all the problems.

9. SOCIAL STUDIES BEAT YOURSELF: Played the same, except the teacher writes a name on the blackboard. The children should find helpful information in their social studies books. Encourage children to use their book indexes, too. Have the children record their own times.

10. DESK BEAT YOURSELF: Played the same, except the children keep a daily record of the time it takes them to completely clean and organize their desks.

11. "Beat Yourself" can be applied to other research skills, such as looking up words in the dictionary, encyclopedias, and so on.

A Record of My Adding Time	
Sept. 17	1 min. - 2 sec.
Sept. 19	1 min.
Sept. 23	1 min.
Sept. 24	55 sec.
Sept. 27	50 sec.
Oct. 2	48 sec.
Oct. 4	48 sec.

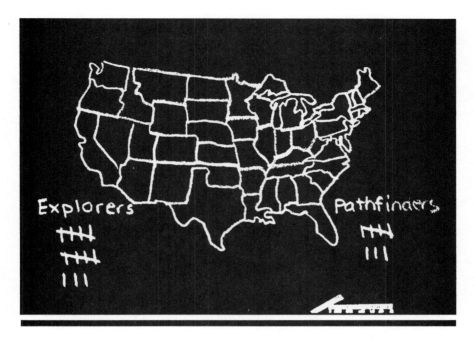

TOURIST

An Intermediate-Grade Game for Social Studies

1. GEOGRAPHY TOURIST: Divide the class into two equal teams, the Explorers and the Pathfinders.

2. If there are thirty children in the classroom, the players on each team are given numbers from one to fifteen. There will be two ones, two twos, two threes, and so on.

3. The teacher pulls down the wall map and names a location on the map. He or she then calls out a number from one to fifteen.

4. The pair of children whose number was called race to point out the location on the map.

5. HISTORY TOURIST: Played the same except the teacher asks a historical question. For example, "What State was Abraham Lincoln born in?" or "Where did Paul Revere make his famous ride?" Children race to point out the answer on the map .

6. This game can be even more interesting if a blank map is drawn on the blackboard. Children must then point to approximate locations of geographical points.

POST OFFICE

An Intermediate-Grade Game for Language and Math

1. POST OFFICE: Two blank envelopes are drawn on the blackboard.

2. Divide the class into two teams. Each team should line up in front of a drawing.

3. The teacher's starting signal is "We want to send a letter to Mary Brown, 123 Magnolia Street, Denver, CO 90220."

4. The first child in line starts writing one word or number and the proper punctuation on the blank envelope. After writing a word or number, the child must return to the end of his or her line and give the next child a turn. Each child is responsible for punctuation near his or her word or number.

5. The first line to correctly finish addressing the envelope wins the game. Guidelines for addressing a letter should be discussed with the class before this activity.

6. This game can be applied to learning formats for other written materials, such as business letters, invitations, and so on.

7. MATH BANKER: Played the same, except the children fill in the missing information on blank checks, inventory lists, receipts, and so on.

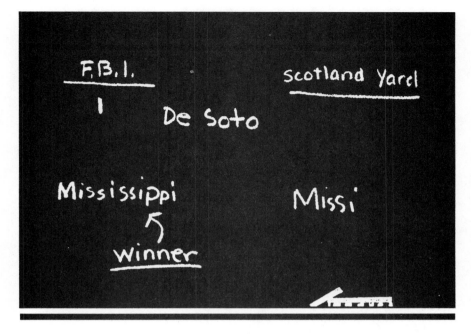

BLACKBOARD SLEUTH

An Intermediate-Grade Game for the Table of Contents, Index, Dictionary, Encyclopedia, Bibliography, and Footnotes

1. INDEX SLEUTH: Divide the class into two teams, Scotland Yard and the F.B.I.

2. Give the children on each team numbers. If there are thirty children in the room, Scotland Yard and the F.B.I. will each have numbers from one to fifteen. In short, there will be two ones in the room, two twos, two threes, and so on.

3. Have the children take out their social studies books.

4. The teacher stands at the front of the class with his or her social studies book open. He or she now gives the following index clue: "I am thinking of the river that was discovered by a man named DeSoto." The teacher writes the name DeSoto on the blackboard.

5. The children immediately start searching their book indexes for the name DeSoto, they find the page number, turn to the page, and locate the name of the river.

6. The teacher must only give clues to mystery names that can be found in the book used by the class.

7. The teacher should wait until most of the children are looking up the answer. Then he or she calls out a number from one to fifteen.

8. The two sevens from Scotland Yard and the F.B.I. race to the board with their answers. The first "sleuth" to write the correctly spelled answer wins a point for his or her team.

9. The game continues as the teacher gives the class another index clue.

10. TABLE OF CONTENTS SLEUTH: Played the same, except the children are only allowed to refer to the table of contents of their social studies books. For example, the teacher says, "I am thinking of the river described in chapter 22 of part 4."

11. DICTIONARY SLEUTH: The teacher gives the children a word to look up in their dictionaries. Children race to the board where they write the word and correctly divide it into syllables or write the word and the definition.

12. ENCYCLOPEDIA SLEUTH: Played the same, except the children are encouraged to use encyclopedias to locate the answers. For example, the teachers says, "I am thinking of the river discovered by DeSoto."

13. BIBLIOGRAPHY SLEUTH: Played the same, except children are only allowed to use the bibliography of a certain book, such as a science textbook. Teacher says, "I am thinking of the year that Dr. Priddle wrote his book, *Itchy Insects*." Children race through their bibliographies to locate the date.

14. FOOTNOTE SLEUTH: Teacher says, "I am thinking of the book that was quoted on page 54 of your books." Children race to find the footnote that gives the title of the book.

15. Needless to say, games described in steps 13 and 14 cannot be played unless all of the children have books with bibliographies and footnotes.

HOUSEHOLD SLEUTH

An Intermediate-Grade Game for Recipe Books, Telephone Books, Newspaper, and Magazine Research

1. HOUSEHOLD SLEUTH: This game is played the same as the game "Blackboard Sleuth" on page 45, except that the research is limited to household literature.

2. Divide the class into two teams, F.B.I. and Scotland Yard.

3. Ask children to bring their own reference materials from home, such as telephone books, newspapers, magazines, recipe books, and so on.

4. NEWSPAPER GAME: Played the same, as "Blackboard Sleuth" on page 45, except that children refer to newspapers. Teacher says, "I am wondering what time I can listen to the news on television tonight." Children race to find the answer in their newspapers. Other sections that can be referred to are births; want ads; weather; local, national, and international news; sports events; entertainment; and so on.

5. RECIPE GAME: Played the same, as "Blackboard Sleuth" on page 45, except children refer to recipe books. Ask children to bring one recipe book from home. Teacher says, "I wonder how many tablespoons are in a cup."

6. TELEPHONE GAME: Played the same, except children refer to telephone books. Teacher says, "I want to phone Donald Darkle but I don't know his phone number." Guidelines on how to use a phone book should be discussed with the class before this activity. Reference can also be made to locating addresses and classified sections of the phone books. Give children opportunities to work with the white and yellow pages.